The Ultimate Compendium of Carl Jung's Best Sayings: A Quotes Reference Book

Joseph Marty

Carl Jung

Copyrights

First edition April 2022

Preface

This book is a small compendium with +450 of the best of Carl Jung's psychological, philosophical, bright observations. Short and compact bursts of his great knowledge, broaden your perspective by incorporating them in your daily life to develop your own unique and special character!

Random Picks

"Everyone can afford to give away a smile."

"We need more understanding of human nature, because the only real danger that exists is man himself."

"The foundation of all mental illness is the unwillingness to experience legitimate suffering."

Carl Gustav Jung (born 26 July 1875 – died 6 June 1961) was a Swiss therapist and psychoanalyst who founded analytic psychology (logical brain research). His work influenced a variety of fields: psychiatry, anthropology, archaeology, literature, philosophy, psychology, and religious studies.

Jung's psychiatric approach (analytical psycology) was distinguished by a focus on the role of symbolic experiences in human life, taking a prospective approach to the issues presented in therapy.

Carl Jung used four psychological functions: thinking, feeling, sensation, and intuition (rational and irrational functions). In addition, he distinguished between the two fundamental life attitudes known as: introversion and extraversion.

This book is a great compilation of his best sayings, top one-liners, and wisest quotes & proverbs. It is a collection of his wisdom, and general world views in different topics: psychiatry, literature, philosophy, life, religion, leadership, success, and so much more.

Quotes

1. “You are what you do, not what you say you’ll do.”

---

2. “Until you make the unconscious conscious, it will direct your life and you will call it fate.”

---

3. “Thinking is difficult, that’s why most people judge.”

---

4. “I am not what happened to me, I am what I choose to become.”

---

5. “What you resist, persists.”

---

6. "Knowing your own darkness is the best method for dealing with the darknesses of other people."

7. "The privilege of a lifetime is to become who you truly are."

8. "Your visions will become clear only when you can look into your own heart. Who looks outside, dreams; who looks inside, awakes."

9. "No tree, it is said, can grow to heaven unless its roots reach down to hell."

10. "I must also have a dark side if I am to be whole."

11. "Everything that irritates us about others can lead us to an understanding of ourselves."

12. "The meeting of two personalities is like the contact of two chemical substances: if there is any reaction, both are transformed."

13. "The first half of life is devoted to forming a healthy ego, the second half is going inward and letting go of it."

14. “The best political, social, and spiritual work we can do is to withdraw the projection of our shadow onto others.”

15. “Even a happy life cannot be without a measure of darkness, and the word happy would lose its meaning if it were not balanced by sadness.”

16. “Every form of addiction is bad, no matter whether the narcotic be alcohol, morphine or idealism.”

17. “Synchronicity is an ever present reality for those who have eyes to see.”

18. “Shame is a soul eating emotion.”

19. “Wholeness is not achieved by cutting off a portion of one’s being, but by integration of the contraries.”

20. “Who looks outside, dreams; who looks inside, awakes.”

21. “As far as we can discern, the sole purpose of human existence is to kindle a light of meaning in the darkness of mere being.”

22. “There is no coming to consciousness without pain. People will do anything, no matter how absurd, in order to avoid facing their own Soul. One does not become enlightened by imagining figures of light, but by making the darkness conscious.”

23. “To ask the right question is already half the solution of a problem.”

---

24. “Life really does begin at forty. Up until then, you are just doing research.”

---

25. “Everyone you meet knows something you don’t know but need to know. Learn from them.”

---

26. “When you are up against a wall, put down roots like a tree, until clarity comes from deeper sources to see over that wall and grow.”

27. “Hurry is not of the devil; hurry is the devil.”

28. “Intuition is perception via the unconscious that brings forth ideas, images, new possibilities and ways out of blocked situations.”

29. “Whatever is rejected from the self, appears in the world as an event.”

30. “The greatest potential for growth and self-realisation exists in the second half of life.”

31. “All fanaticism is repressed doubt.”

32. “Real work is completed in silence and strikes a chord in the minds of only a very few.”

33. “Shadow work is the path of the heart warrior.”

34. “Man cannot stand a meaningless life.”

35. “To confront a person with their own shadow is to show them their own light.”

36. “God enters through the wound.”

37. "One must be able to let things happen."

38. "The pendulum of the mind alternates between sense and nonsense, not between right and wrong."

39. "Perhaps, I myself am the enemy who needs to be loved."

40. "The doctor is effective only when he himself is affected. Only the wounded physician heals."

41. "Called or not, God is always there."

42. "That which you do not bring to consciousness comes to you as your Fate, that which you do bring to consciousness, whether it was what you thought you wanted or not, is your destiny."

43. "Religion is a defense against the experience of God."

44. "Had I left those images hidden in the emotions, I might have been torn to pieces by them."

45. "The least of things with a meaning is worth more in life than the greatest of things without it."

46. "Knowledge rests not upon truth alone, but upon error also."

47. "Faith, hope, love, and insight are the highest achievements of human effort. They are found-given-by experience."

48. “As a child I felt myself to be alone, and I am still, because I know things and must hint at things which others apparently know nothing of, and for the most part do not want to know.”

49. “The healthy man does not torture others – generally it is the tortured who turn into torturers.”

50. “We cannot live the afternoon of life according to the program of life’s morning; for what in the morning was true will in evening become a lie.”

51. “This whole creation is essentially subjective, and the dream is the theater where the dreamer is at once: scene, actor, prompter, stage manager, author, audience, and critic.”

52. “Loneliness does not come from having no people about one, but from being unable to communicate the things that seem important to oneself, or from holding certain views which others find inadmissible.”

53. “We know that the wildest and most moving dramas are played not in the theatre but in the hearts of ordinary men and women.”

54. “Life calls not for perfection, but for completeness.”

55. "How can I be substantial if I do not cast a shadow? I must have a dark side also If I am to be whole."

56. "If a man knows more than others, he becomes lonely."

57. "Do not compare, do not measure. No other way is like yours. All other ways deceive and tempt you. You must fulfill the way that is in you."

58. "Learn your theories as well as you can, but put them aside when you touch the miracle of the living soul."

59. “The most important question anyone can ask is: What myth am I living?”

60. “The psychic depths are nature, and nature is creative life.”

61. “The collective unconscious contains the whole spiritual heritage of mankind’s evolution born anew in the brain structure of every individual.”

62. “I would rather be whole than good.”

63. "Where wisdom reigns, there is no conflict between thinking and feeling."

64. "It all depends on how we look at things, and not how they are in themselves."

65. "A mandala is the psychological expression of the totality of the self."

66. "Life is a luminous pause between two mysteries that are yet one."

67. “The most terrifying thing is to accept oneself completely.”

68. “We don’t get wounded alone and we don’t heal alone.”

69. “We have forgotten the age-old fact that God speaks chiefly through dreams and visions.”

70. “Often the hands will solve a mystery that the intellect has struggled with in vain.”

71. “The greater the contrast, the greater the potential. Great energy only comes from a correspondingly great tension of opposites.”

72. “If our religion is based on salvation, our chief emotions will be fear and trembling. If our religion is based on wonder, our chief emotion will be gratitude.”

73. “Dreams are the guiding words of the Soul.”

74. “To be normal is the ultimate aim of the unsuccessful.”

75. "Summoned or not, the god will come."

76. "The shadow is a moral problem that challenges the whole ego-personality, for no one can become conscious of the shadow without considerable moral effort."

77. "Our unconscious is the key to our life's pursuits."

78. "Individualization does not shut one out from the world, but gathers the world to oneself."

79. “The right way to wholeness is made up of fateful detours and wrong turnings.”

80. “The greatest and most important problems of life are all fundamentally insoluble. They can never be solved but only outgrown.”

81. “The unconscious mind of man sees correctly even when conscious reason is blind and impotent.”

82. “Life is crazy and meaningful at once.”

83. "Man needs difficulties; they are necessary for health."

84. "One finds one's destiny on the path one takes to avoid it."

85. "The dream is the small hidden door in the deepest and most intimate sanctum of the soul..."

86. "The creative mind plays with the object it loves."

87. "The shoe that fits one person pinches another; there is no recipe for living that suits all cases."

88. "The attainment of wholeness requires one to stake one's whole being. Nothing less will do; there can be no easier conditions, no substitutes, no compromises."

89. "Where love stops, power begins, and violence, and terror."

90. "For the alchemist the one primarily in need of redemption is not man, but the deity who is lost and sleeping in matter."

91. "The man who promises everything is sure to fulfil nothing, and everyone who promises too much is in danger of using evil means in order to carry out his promises, and is already on the road to perdition."

92. "The most intense conflicts, if overcome, leave behind a sense of security and calm that is not easily disturbed. It is just these intense conflicts and their conflagration which are needed to produce valuable and lasting results."

93. “Who has fully realized that history is not contained in thick books but lives in our very blood?”

94. “The meaning and design of a problem seem not to lie in its solution, but in our working at it incessantly.”

95. “The separation of psychology from the premises of biology is purely artificial, because the human psyche lives in indissoluble union with the body.”

96. “Find out what a person fears most and that is where he will develop next.”

97. “In sleep, fantasy takes the form of dreams. But in waking life, too, we continue to dream beneath the threshold of consciousness, especially when under the influence of repressed or other unconscious complexes.”

98. “Dawn is born at midnight.”

99. “What we lack is intensity of life.”

100. “Simple things are always the most difficult.”

101. “That which we do not confront in ourselves we will meet as fate.”

102. “Every psychic advance of man arises from the suffering of the soul.”

103. “I believe that history is capable of anything. There exists no folly that men have not tried out.”

104. “The only thing we have to fear on this planet is man.”

---

105. "What is not brought to consciousness, comes to us as fate."

---

106. "Everyone carries a shadow, and the less it is embodied in the individual's conscious life, the blacker and denser it is. At all counts, it forms an unconscious snag, thwarting our most well-meant intentions."

---

107. "What happens after death is so unspeakably glorious that our imagination and our feelings do not suffice to form even an approximate conception of it. The dissolution of our time-bound form in eternity brings no loss of meaning."

108. "Conflicts create the fire of affects and emotions; and like every fire it has two aspects: that of burning and that of giving light."

109. “The acceptance of oneself is the essence of the whole moral problem and the epitome of a whole outlook on life.”

110. “When goals go, meaning goes. When meaning goes, purpose goes. When purpose goes, life goes dead on our hands.”

111. “A complex is a cluster of energy in the unconscious, charged by historic events, reinforced through repitition, embodying a fragment of our personality, and generating a programmed response and an implicit set of expectations.”

112. “Children are educated by what the grown-up is and not by his talk.”

113. “I shall not commit the fashionable stupidity of regarding everything I cannot explain as a fraud.”

114. "The Self then functions as a union of opposites and thus constitutes the most immediate experience of the Divine which it is psychologically possible to imagine."

115. "A dream that is not understood remains a mere occurrence; understood it becomes a living experience."

116. “There is no such thing as a pure extrovert or a pure introvert. Such a man would be in the lunatic asylum.”

117. “Enlightenment doesnt occur from sitting around visualizing images of light, but from integrating the darker aspects of the Self into the conscious personality.”

118. “As a plant produces its flower, so the psyche creates its symbols.”

119. “Masses are always breeding grounds of psychic epidemics.”

120. "Every living soul has different talents, different desires, different faculties. Be yourself, for even if you deceive the entire world, you will be ten thousand times worse than nothing."

121. "To find out what is truly individual in ourselves, profound reflection is needed; and suddenly we realize how uncommonly difficult the discovery of individuality is."

122. “Far from being a material world, this is a psychic world, which allows us to make only indirect and hypothetical inferences about the real nature of matter. The psychic, alone has immediate reality, and this includes all forms of the psychic, even.”

123. “The maintenance of secrets acts like a psychic poison which alienates the possessor from the community.”

124. "I don't aspire to be a good man. I aspire to be a whole man."

125. "Understanding does not cure evil, but it is a definite help, inasmuch as one can cope with a comprehensible darkness."

126. "A creative person has little power over his own life. He is not free. He is captive and driven by his daimon."

127. "Enchantment is the oldest form of medicine."

“The artist is not a person endowed with free will who seeks his own
128. ends, but one who allows it to realize its supreme purpose through him.”

“A sense of a wider meaning to one’s existence is what raises a
129. man beyond mere getting and spending. If he lacks this sense, he is lost and miserable.”

130. "But we must not forget that only a very few people are artists in life; that the art of life is the most distinguished and rarest of all the arts."

---

131. "Real liberation comes not from glossing over or repressing painful states of feeling, but only from experiencing them to the full."

“I am looking forward enormously to getting back to the sea again,

132. where the overstimulated psyche can recover in the presence of that infinite peace and spaciousness.”

“We are a psychic process which we do not control, or only partly

133. direct. Consequently, we cannot have any final judgment about ourselves or our lives.”

134. "Deeply listening to music opens up new avenues of research I'd never even dreamed of. I feel from now on music should be an essential part of every analysis."

135. "The experience of the self is always a defeat for the ego."

136. "You always become the thing you fight the most."

137. "I could not say I believe. I know! I have had the experience of being gripped by something that is stronger than myself, something that people call God."

138. "When you come to think about it, nothing has any meaning, for when there was nobody to think, there was nobody to interpret what happened."

“It is just man’s turning away from instinct – his opposing himself to instinct – that creates
139. consciousness. Instinct is nature andseeks to perpetuate nature; while consciousness can only seek culture or its denial.”

“The psychopathology of the
140. masses is rooted in the psychology of the individual.”

“It is a fact that cannot be denied: the wickedness of others becomes
141. our own wickedness because it kindles something evil in our own hearts.”

“Every man carries within himself the eternal image of woman, not the image of this or that particular
142. woman, but a definite feminine image. This image is fundamentally unconscious, a hereditary factor of primordial origin.”

143. "Man is in need if a symbolical life- badly in need. We only live banal, ordinary, rational or irrational things- but we have no symbolic life. Where do we live symbolically? Nowhere except where we participate in the ritual of life."

144. "The unconscious psyche believes in life after death."

145. "The longing for light is the longing for consciousness."

146. "Nothing is possible without love."

147. "One could say, with a little exaggeration, that the persona is that which in reality one is not, but which oneself as well as others think one is."

148. "Neurosis is an inner cleavage-the state of being at war with oneself."

149. "A true symbol appears only when there is a need to express what thought cannot think or what is only divined or felt."

150. "An old man who cannot bid farewell to life appears as feeble and sickly as the young man who is unable to embrace it."

151. "Science has destroyed even the refuge of the inner life. What was once a sheltering haven has become a place of terror."

152. "It is only our deeds that reveal who we are."

153. "My evenings are taken up very largely with astrology. I make horoscopic calculations in order to find a clue to the core of psychological truth."

154. "No man can change himself into anything from sheer reason; he can only change into what he potentially is."

“The distinction between mind and body is an artificial dichotomy, a discrimination which is

155. unquestionably based far more on the peculiarity of intellectual understanding than on the nature of things.”

“The general function of dreams is to try to restore our psychological balance by producing dream

156. material that re-establishes, in a subtle way, the total psychic equilibrium.”

157. “One cannot live without inconsistency.”

---

158. “The judgment of the intellect is, at best, only the half of truth.”

---

159. “What was given to us by the past is adapted to the possibilities of the future.”

---

160. “Because the European does not know his own unconscious, he does not understand the East and projects it into everything he fears and despises in himself.”

161. “Nature does not deceive or conceal, but reveals.”

162. “People are never helped in their suffering by what they think for themselves, but only by revelation of a wisdom greater than their own. It is this which lifts them out of their distress.”

163. “The symbol in the dream has more the value of a parable: it does not conceal, it teaches.”

164. "To this day God is the name by which I designate all things which cross my willful path violently and recklessly, all things which upset my subjective views, plans and intentions and change the course of my life for better or worse."

165. "Liverpool is the pool of life, it makes to live."

166. "In order to know the light, we must first experience the darkness."

167. "The most dangerous things in the world are immense accumulations of human beings who are manipulated by only a few heads."

168. "Freedom stretches only as far as the limits of our consciousness."

169. "Without freedom there can be no morality."

170. "Much of the evil in the world is due to the fact that man in general is hopelessly unconscious."

171. "What usually has the strongest psychic effect on the child is the life which the parents have not lived."

172. "Sometimes a tree tells you more than can be read in books."

173. "Every Mother contains her daughter in herself and every daughter her mother and every mother extends backwards into her mother and forwards into her daughter."

174. "The gods have become our diseases."

175. “Our intellect has created a new world that dominates nature, and has populated it with monstrous machines.”

---

176. “To me dreams are part of nature, which harbors no intention to deceive but expresses something as best it can.”

---

177. “To the critical intelligence, nothing is left of absolute reality.”

---

178. “To make what fate intends for me my own intention.”

179. "Man positively needs general ideas and convictions that will give a meaning to his life and enable him to find a place for himself in the universe."

180. "An archetypal content expresses itself, first and foremost, in metaphors."

181. "I could well imagine that I might have lived in former centuries and there encountered questions I was not yet able to answer; that I had been born again because I had not fulfilled the task given to me."

182. "Our psyche is set up in accord with the structure of the universe, and what happens in the macrocosm likewise happens in the infinitesimal and most subjective reaches of the psyche."

183. …iatrists classify a person as neurotic if he suffers from his problems in living, and a psychotic if he makes others suffer.”

184. “One is always in the dark about one’s own personality. One needs others to get to know oneself.”

185. “Criticism can be effective when there is something that must be destroyed or dissolved, but it is capable only of harm when there is something to be built.”

186. “Nobody doubts the importance of conscious experience; why then should we doubt the significance of unconscious happenings? They also are part of our life, and sometimes more truly a part of it for weal or woe than any happenings of the day.”

---

187. “Twelve experts gathered in one room equal one big idiot.”

---

188. “The sure path can only lead to death.”

---

189. “No nation keeps its word. A nation is a big, blind worm, following what? Fate perhaps. A nation has no honor, it has no word to keep .”

190. “A residual sea of symbols which is shared by all mankind, usually accessed through dreams or altered states, and from which cultures draw images on which to found their religions.”

191. “It is often tragic to see how blatantly a man bungles his own life and the lives of others yet remains totally incapable of seeing how much the whole tragedy originates in himself, and how he continually feeds it and keeps it going.”

192. "No matter what the world thinks about religious experience, the one who has it possesses a great treasure, a thing that has become for him a source of life, meaning, and beauty, and that has given a new splendor to the world and to mankind."

193. "The debt we owe to the play of imagination is incalculable."

194. “Primitive superstition lies just below the surface of even the most tough-minded individuals, and it is precisely those who most fight against it who are the first to succumb to its suggestive effects.”

195. “Our intellect has achieved the most tremendous things, but in the meantime our spiritual dwelling has fallen into disrepair.”

196. “The man of today, who resembles more or less the collective ideal, has made his heart into a den of murderers, as can easily be proved by the analysis of his unconscious, even though he himself is not in the least disturbed by it.”

197. “Healing proceeds from the depths to the heights.”

198. “In such doubtful matters, where you have to work as a pioneer, you must be able to put some trust in your intuition and follow your feeling even at the risk of going wrong.”

199. “Error is just as important a condition of life’s progress as truth.”

200. “Eternal truth needs a human language that alters with the spirit of the times.”

201. “What you call knowledge is an attempt to impose something comprehensible on life.”

202. “Dreams are the facts from which we must proceed.”

203. “A special ability means a heavy expenditure of energy in a particular direction, with a consequent drain from some other side of life.”

“And what shall we know of this life on earth after death? The dissolution of our timebound form
204. in eternity brings no loss of meaning. Rather, does the little finger know itself a member of the hand.”

“I find that all my thoughts circle around God like the planets around the sun, and are as irresistibly
205. attracted by Him. I would feel it to be the grossest sin if I were to oppose any resistance to this force.”

---

206. "The angel personifies something new arising from the deep unconscious."

---

207. "The whole nature of man presupposes woman, both physically and spiritually. His system is tuned into woman from the start, just as it is prepared for a quite definite world where there is water, light, air, salt, carbohydrates etc..."

208. “Becoming conscious is of course a sacrilege against nature; it is as though you had robbed the unconscious of something.”

209. “Nothing is more repulsive than a furtively prurient spirituality; it is just as unsavory as gross sensuality.”

210. "God has fallen out of containment in religion and into human hearts – God is incarnating. Our whole unconscious is in an uproar from the God Who wants to know and to be known."

211. "Creativity is the art that can give rise to visionary metaphorical relationships, as opposed to purely psy-chological ones."

212. “It is a moral achievement on the part of the doctor who ought not to let himself be repelled by sickness and corruption.”

---

213. “My whole being was seeking for something still unknown which might confer meaning upon the banality of life.”

---

214. “There is a deep need in the world just now for guidance – almost any sort of spiritual guidance.”

215. “Remember that the only God man comes in contact with is his own God, called Spirit, Soul and Mind, or Consciousness, and these three are one.”

216. “Art is a kind of innate drive that seizes a human being and makes him its instrument...”

217. “Modern man is battered by the fundamental forces of his own psyche.”

218. “The conscious mind allows itself to be trained like a parrot, but the unconscious does not – which is why St. Augustine thanked God for not making him responsible for his dreams.”

219. “But India did not pass me by without a trace: it left tracks which lead me from one infinity to another infinity.”

220. "A book of mine is always a matter of fate. There is something unpredictable about the process of writing, and I cannot prescribe for myself any predetermined course."

221. "About a third of my cases are suffering from no clinically definable neurosis, but from the senselessness and emptiness of their lives. This can be defined as the general neurosis of our times."

222. “Creative powers can just as easily turn out to be destructive. It rests solely with the moral personality whether they apply themselves to good things or to bad. And if this is lacking, no teacher can supply it or take its place.”

223. “Even a lie is a psychic fact.”

224. “When one is not understood one should as a rule lower one’s voice, because when one really speaks loudly enough and is not heard, it is because people do not want to hear. One had better begin to mutter to oneself, then they get curious.”

---

225. “The psyche is a natural phenomenon. All aspects of the psyche, even those which seem pathological or destructive, actually serve the function of furthering our psychological development.”

226. "Everything psychic is pregnant with the future."

227. "His retreat into himself is not a final renunciation of the world, but a search for quietude, where alone it is possible for him to make his contribution to the life of the community."

228. "To become acquainted with oneself is a terrible shock."

229. “The angels are a strange genus, they are precisely what they are and cannot be anything else. They are themselves soul-less beings who represent nothing but the thoughts and intuitions of their Lord.”

230. “The more veiled becomes the outside world, steadily losing in colour, tone and passions, the more urgently the inner world calls us.”

231. “Our whole educational problem suffers from a one-sided approach to the child who is to be educated, and from an equally one-sided lack of emphasis on the uneducatedness of the educator.”

232. “Our heart glows, and secret unrest gnaws at the root of our being. Dealing with the unconscious has become a question of life for us.”

233. “From the middle of life onward, only he remains vitally alive who is ready to die with life.”

234. “The creative process is a living thing, implanted, as it were in the souls of men.”

235. “All the works of man have their origin in creative fantasy. What right have we then to depreciate imagination.”

236. “Hitler’s movement is near to Mohammedanism.”

237. “If you should see people in a room, you would not think that you had made those people, or that you were responsible for them.”

238. “Continuous creation is to be thought of not only as a series of successive acts of creation, but also as the eternal presence of the one creative act.”

239. “The individual disposition is already a factor in childhood; it is innate, and not acquired in the course of a life.”

“All my writings may be considered tasks imposed from within, their source was a fateful compulsion.

240. What I wrote were things that assailed me from within myself. I permitted the spirit that moved me to speak out.”

“Only in our creative acts do we

241. step forth into the light and see ourselves whole and complete.”

---

242. “A collection of a hundred great brains makes one big fathead.”

---

243. “The afternoon of a human life must have a significance of its own, and cannot be merely a pitiful appendage to life’s morning.”

244. “How difficult it is to reach anything approaching a moderate and relatively calm point of view in the midst of one’s emotions.”

245. “During my medical education at the University of Basle I found vivisection horrible, barbarous and above all unnecessary.”

246. “Protection and security are only valuable if they do not cramp life excessively.”

247. “Doesn’t the world bring forth thinking in human heads with the same necessity that it brings forth blossoms on the plant?”

248. “I want to be freed neither from human beings, nor from myself, nor from nature; for all these appear to me the greatest of miracles.”

"There was need of a phantastic,
indestructible optimism, and one
far removed from all sense of
249. reality, in order, for example, to
discover in the shameful death of
Christ really the highest salvation
and the redemption of the world."

"The wine of youth does not always
250. clear with advancing years;
sometimes it grows turbid."

251. “Only a few individuals succeed in throwing off mythology in a time of a certain intellectual supremacy – the mass never frees itself.”

252. “For, in order to turn the individual into a function of the State, his dependence on anything beside the State must be taken from him.”

253. "I have always been impressed by the fact that there are a surprising number of individuals who never use their minds if they can avoid it, and an equal number who do use their minds, but in an amazingly stupid way."

254. "Fortunately, in her kindness and patience, Nature has never put the fatal question as to the meaning of their lives into the mouths of most people. And where no one asks, no one needs to answer."

255. "Wherever an inferiority complex exists, there is a good reason for it."

256. "Too much of the animal disfigures the civilized human being, too much culture makes a sick animal."

257. "Ultimate truth, if there be such a thing, demands the concert of many voices."

258. "If you are unhappy, you are too high up in your mind."

259. "Whenever we give up, leave behind, and forget too much, there is always the danger that the things we have neglected will return with added force."

260. "One of the most difficult tasks men can perform, however much others may despise it, is the invention of good games."

261. "Nobody, as long as he moves about among the chaotic currents of life, is without trouble."

262. “An understanding heart is everything in a teacher, and cannot be esteemed highly enough.”

263. “Whatever is not conscious will be experienced as fate.”

264. “Hitler is a medicine man type of leader.”

265. “Gnosticism was stamped out completely and its remnants are so badly mangled that special study is needed to get any insight at all into its inner meaning.”

266. “I have frequently seen people become neurotic when they content themselves with inadequate or wrong answers to the questions of life.”

267. “Yoga in Mayfair or Fifth Avenue, or in any other place which is on the telephone, is a spiritual fake.”

268. “Hitler is a shy and friendly man with artistic tastes and gifts.”

269. “Hitler’s unconscious seems to be female.”

270. "St. Thomas is really a great man quite apart from his saintliness."

"The secret of artistic creation and the effectiveness of art is to be found in a return to the state of

271. 'participation mystique' – to that level of experience at which it is man who lives, and not the individual..."

---

272. "One is forced to speak not of what is held in common between the cultures, but what is held in common between the myths, and that in its simplest archetypal forms."

273. "What happens in the life of Christ happens always and everywhere. In the Christian archetype all lives of this kind are prefigured."

274. "One cannot free oneself by bowing to the yoke, but by breaking it."

275. “The mind has grown to its present state of consciousness as an acorn grows into an oak, or as saurians developed into mammals.”

276. “The Wrong we have Done, Thought, or Intended Will wreak its Vengeance on Our SOULS.”

277. “Plato’s world of ideas is beautiful.”

278. “The unconscious is the unwritten history of mankind from time unrecorded.”

279. “When religion stops talking about animals it will be all downhill.”

280. “However far-fetched it may sound, experience shows that many neuroses are caused by the fact that people blind themselves to their own religious promptings because of a childish passion for rational enlightenment.”

281. “Psychological type is nothing static – it changes in the course of life.”

282. “The unsatisfied yearning of the artist reaches back to the primordial image in the unconscious which is best fitted to compensate the inadequacy and one-sidedness of the present.”

---

283. “We often dream about people from whom we receive a letter by the next post. I have ascertained on several occasions that at the moment when the dream occurred the letter was already lying in the post-office of the addressee.”

---

284. "Man is the mirror God holds up to himself, the sense organ with which he apprehends his being."

---

285. "To become conscious of it involves recognizing the dark aspects of the personality as present and real."

---

286. "Mind and matter are two different aspects of one and the same thing."

---

287. "Science is the tool of the Western mind and with it more doors can be opened than with bare hands."

---

288. "I am the triple owner of the world, the finest Turkey, the Lorelei, Germania and Helvetia of exclusively sweet butter and Naples, and I must supply the whole world with macaroni."

289. "Whoever is afraid must needs be dependent; a weak thing needs support. That is why the primitive mind, from deep psychological necessity, begot religious instruction and embodied it in a magician or a priest."

290. "Imagination is a concentrated extract of all the forces of life."

---

291. "I believe that we have no real access to who we really are except in God. Only when we rest in God can we find the safety, the spaciousness, and the scary freedom to be who we are, all that we are, more than we are, and less than we are."

"Thanks to the acuteness of his mind, he saw through the poverty
292. of philosophical and Gnostic knowledge, and contemptuously rejected it."

"I have treated many hundreds of patients. Among those in the second half of life – that is to say,
293. over 35 – there has not been one whose problem in the last resort was not that of finding a religious outlook on life."

---

294. "Only a life lived in a certain spirit is worth living. It is a remarkable fact that a life lived entirely from the ego is dull not only for the person himself but for all concerned."

295. "Special knowledge is a terrible disadvantage."

296. "Creative power is mightier than its possessor."

297. "My work as a psychoanalyst is to help patients recover their lost wholeness and to strengthen the psyche so it can resist future dismemberment."

298. "The dream arises from a part of the mind unknown to us, but none the less important, and is concerned with the desires for the approaching day."

299. "I think that one should view with philosophic admiration the strange paths of the libido and should investigate the purposes of its circuitous ways."

300. "Synchronistic events provide an immediate religious experience as a direct encounter with the compensatory patterning of events in nature as a whole, both inwardly and outwardly."

301. "Even a happy life cannot be without a measure of darkness."

302. "The majority of my patients consisted not of believers but of those who had lost their faith."

---

303. "Life calls us forth to independence, and anyone who does not heed this call because of childish laziness or timidity is threatened with neurosis. And once this has broken out, it becomes an increasingly valid reason for running away from life..."

“In my case Pilgrim’s Progress
consisted in my having to climb
304. down a thousand ladders until I
could reach out my hand to the
little clod of earth that I am.”

“When you walk with naked feet,
305. how can you ever forget the
Earth?”

“Only by discovering alchemy have I clearly understood that the Unconscious is a process and that

306. ego’s rapport with the Unconscious and its contents initiate an evolution, more precisely, a real metamorphosis of the psyche.”

“You can take away a man’s gods,

307. but only to give him others in return.”

308. “Language, in its origin and essence, is simply a system of signs or symbols that denote real occurrences or their echo in the human soul.”

309. “Every civilized human being, whatever his conscious development, is still an archaic man at the deeper levels of his psyche.”

310. “I had to make a confession of faith in stone. That was the beginning of the tower, the house I built for myself at Bollingen.”

311. “Once upon a time men were possessed by devils. Now they are not less obsessed by ideas.”

312. “Colors express the main psychic functions of man.”

313. “The brain is viewed as an appendage of the genital glands.”

314. “Myth is more individual and expresses life more precisely than does science.”

“At times I feel as if I am spread out over the landscape and inside things, and am myself living in

315. every tree, in the plashing of the waves, in the clouds and the animals that come and go, in the procession of the seasons.”

---

316. “Never do human beings speculate more, or have more opinions, than about things which they do not understand.”

---

317. "The starry vault of heaven is in truth the open book of cosmic projection..."

318. "You can expect no influence if you are not susceptible to influence."

319. "Dream the dream onward."

320. "The squaring of the circle is a stage on the way to the unconscious, a point of transition leading to a goal lying as yet unformulated beyond it. It is one of those paths to the centre."

321. “The cinema, like the detective story, makes it possible to experience without danger all the excitement, passion and desirousness which must be repressed in a humanitarian ordering of life.”

---

322. “Sensation tell us a thing is. Thinking tell us what it is this thing is. Feeling tells us what this thing is to us.”

323. "The spirit is the life of the body seen from within, and the body the outward manifestation of the life of the spirit-the two being really one."

324. "People cannot stand too much Reality."

325. "Consciousness succumbs all too easily to unconscious influences, and these are often truer and wiser than our conscious thinking."

326. "One of the main functions of formalized religion is to protect people against a direct experience of God."

327. "Paul hardly ever allows the real Jesus of Nazareth to get a word in."

328. "No concept is a carrier of life."

329. "The images of the unconscious place a great responsibility upon a man. Failure to understand them, or a shirking of ethical responsibility, deprives him of his wholeness and imposes a painful fragmentariness on his life."

330. "Explore daily the will of God."

331. "Most of our difficulties come from losing contact with our instincts, with the age-old forgotten wisdom stored up in us."

332. “We are born at a given moment, in a given place and, like vintage years of wine, we have the qualities of the year and of the season of which we are born. Astrology does not lay claim to anything more.”

333. “We do not know whether Hitler is going to found a new Islam. He is already on the way; he is like Mohammad. The emotion in Germany is Islamic; warlike and Islamic. They are all drunk with wild god. That can be the historic future.”

334. "Music is the application of sounds to the canvas of silence."

335. "The word 'belief' is a difficult thing for me. I don't believe. I must have a reason for a certain hypothesis. Either I know a thing, and then I know it – I don't need to believe it."

336. "Life is teleology par excellence; it is the intrinsic striving towards a goal, and the living organism is a system of directed aims which seek to fulfill themselves."

337. "Modern man is sick because he is not whole."

338. "A man's hatred is always concentrated upon that which makes him conscious of his bad qualities."

339. "All neurotics seek the religious."

340. "Meaninglessnes s inhibits fullness of life and is therefore the equivalent to illness. Meaning makes a great many things endurable – perh aps everything."

341. "Not nature, but the genius of mankind,"

342. "It is sad but unfortunately true that man learns nothing from history."

343. "He who looks without, dreams; he who looks within, awakes."

344. "Instinct is like Nature herself – prodigiously conservative, and yet transcending her own historical conditions in her acts of creation."

345. "When an individual does not become conscious of their inner contradictions, the world acts out the conflict and is torn in opposite halves."

346. "Between the dreams of night and day there is not so great a difference."

347. "The world hangs on a thin thread, and that is the psyche of man."

348. "In the final analysis, we count for something only because of the essential that we embody. If we do not embody that, life is wasted."

349. "Good does not become better by being exaggerated, but worse; And a small evil becomes a big one through being disregarded and repressed."

350. "When facts are few, speculations are most likely to represent individual psychology."

"The self as the essence of
individuality is unitemporal and
351. unique; as an archetypal symbol it
is a God-image and therefore
universal and eternal."

"Through pride we are ever
deceiving ourselves. But deep down
352. below the surface of the average
conscience a still, small voice says
to us, something is out of tune."

353. "Man and woman become a devil to each other when they do not separate their spiritual paths, for the nature of created beings is always the nature of differentiation."

---

354. "No dream symbol can be separated from the individual who dreams it, and there is no definite or straightforward interpretation of any dream."

---

355. "Words are animals, alive with a will of their own."

356. “The apparently unendurable conflict is proof of the rightness of your life. A life without contradiction is only half a life; or else a life in the Beyond, which is destined only for angels. But God loves human beings more than the angels.”

357. “Water is the commonest symbol for the unconscious.”

358. "Dreams are symbolic in order that they cannot be understood; in order that the wish, which is the source of the dream, may remain unknown."

359. "Shrinking away from death is something unhealthy and abnormal which robs the second half of life of its purpose."

“From the viewpoint of analytic psychology, the theatre, aside from
360. any aesthetic value, may be considered as an institution for the treatment of the mass complex.”

361. “Thank God I’m not a Jungian.”

“Like the sea itself, the unconscious yields an endless and self-
362. replenishing abundance of creatures, a wealth beyond our fathoming.”

363. “If only simplicity were not the most difficult of all things. It consists of watching objectively the development of any fragment of fantasy.”

364. “The symbols of the self arise from the depths of the body.”

365. “The more uncertain I have felt about myself, the more there has grown up in me a feeling of kinship with all things.”

366. “Sentimentality is a superstructure covering brutality.”

367. “It was most essential for me to have a normal life in the real world as a counterpoise to that strange inner world. My family and my profession remained the base to which I could return...”

---

368. “If one does not understand a person, one tends to regard him as a fool.”

---

369. “There can be no transforming of darkness into light and of apathy into movement without emotion.”

370. “Please remember, it is what you are that heals, not what you know.”

371. “Enlightenment consists not merely in the seeing of luminous shapes and visions, but in making the darkness visible. The latter procedure is more difficult and therefore, unpopular.”

372. “The true leader is always led.”

373. “I live in my deepest hell and from there I cannot fall any further.”

374. "Nights through dreams tell the myths forgotten by the day."

375. "The Christian missionary may preach the gospel to the poor naked heathen, but the spiritual heathen who populate Europe have as yet heard nothing of Christianity."

376. "Commendation heals; condemnation destroys."

377. "Only the wounded physician heals."

378. "For better to come, good must stand aside."

379. "Without this playing with fantasy no creative work has ever yet come to birth. The debt we owe to the play of the imagination is incalculable."

380. “Archetypes, in spite of their conservative nature, are not static but in a continuous dramatic flux. Thus the self as a monad or continuous unit would be dead. But it lives inasmuch as it splits and unites again. There is no energy without opposites!”

381. “We all must do what Christ did. We must make our experiment. We must make mistakes. We must live out our own version of life. And there will be error. If you avoid error you do not live.”

382. "In fact, the whole of mythology could be taken as a sort of projection of the collective unconscious."

383. "It is a bewildering thing in human life that the things that cause the greatest fear is the source of the greatest wisdom."

384. "The man who speaks with primordial images, speaks with a thousand tongues."

385. "Follow that will and that way which experience confirms to be your own."

386. "The greater the tension, the greater is the potential."

387. "In the history of the collective as in the history of the individual, everything depends on the development of consciousness."

388. “My own understanding is the sole treasure I possess, and the greatest. Though infinitely small and fragile in comparison with the powers of darkness, it is still a light, my only light.”

389. “The inner man has access to the sense organs of god.”

390. “Solitude is for me a fount of healing which makes my life worth living.”

391. “The psychiatrist knows only too well how each of us becomes the helpless but not pitiable victim of his own sentiments. Sentimentality is the superstructure erected upon brutality.”

392. “The self is not only the centre but also the whole circumference which embraces both conscious and unconscious; it is the centre of this totality, just as the ego is the centre of consciousness.”

393. "In the products of the unconscious we discover mandala symbols, that is, circular and quaternity figures which express wholeness, and whenever we wish to express wholeness, we employ just such figures."

394. "All art intuitively apprehends coming changes in the collective unconsciousness."

395. "A man who has not passed through the inferno of his passions has never overcome them."

396. “We should not pretend to understand the world only by the intellect. The judgement of the intellect is only part of the truth.”

397. “The bigger the crowd, the more negligible the individual.”

398. “We discover ourselves through others.”

399. “Magic is the science of the jungle.”

400. “Nobody can fall so low unless he has a great depth. If such a thing can happen to a man, it challenges his best and highest on the other side; that is to say, this depth corresponds to a potential height, and the blackest darkness to a hidden light.”

401. “Sometimes you have to do something unforgivable just to be able to go on living.”

402. “I’ve realized that somebody who’s tired and needs a rest, and goes on working all the same is a fool.”

403. “I am no longer alone with myself, and I can only artificially recall the scary and beautiful feeling of solitude. This is the shadow side of the fortune of love.”

404. “Neurosis is the suffering of a soul which has not discovered its meaning.”

405. "Seldom, or perhaps never, does a marriage develop into an individual relationship smoothly and without crises; there is no coming to consciousness without pain."

406. "A particularly beautiful woman is a source of terror. As a rule, a beautiful woman is a terrible disappointment."

407. "In each of us is another whom we do not know. He speaks to us in dreams and tells us how differently he sees us from the way we see ourselves."

408. "Man's task is to become conscious of the contents that press upward from the unconscious."

409. "Fidelity to the law of your own being is an act of high courage flung in the face of life."

410. "The greatest sin is to be unconscious."

411. “Nature is not matter only. She is also a spirit.”

412. “We don’t really heal anything; we simply let it go.”

413. “Every human life contains a potential, if that potential is not fulfilled, then that life was wasted...”

414. “Our world has become dehumanized. Man feels himself isolated in the cosmos, because he is no longer involved in nature.”

415. "The upheaval of our world and the upheaval of our consciousness are one and the same."

416. "Individuation is to divest the self of false wrappings."

417. "The symbols of the self arise in the depths of the body, and they express its materiality every bit as much as the perceiving consciousness. The symbol is thus a living body."

418. “Intuition does not denote something contrary to reason, but something outside of the province of reason.”

419. “Conflict exists strictly as an opportunity to raise our consciousness.”

420. “Recognition of the reality of evil necessarily relativizes the good, and the evil likewise, converting both into halves of a paradoxical whole.”

“The reason for evil in the world is
421. that people are not able to tell their
stories.”

“But, if you have nothing at all to
422. create, then perhaps you create
yourself.”

“The whole point of Jesus’s life was
not that we should become exactly
like him, but that we should become
423. ourselves in the same way he
became himself. Jesus was not the
great exception but the great
example.”

424. “Show me a sane man and I will cure him for you.”

425. “The descent into the depths always seems to precede the ascent.”

426. “Synchronicity reveals the meaningful connections between the subjective and objective world.”

427. “When an inner situation is not made conscious, it appears outside as fate.”

428. “Astrology is assured of recognition from psychology, without further restrictions, because astrology represents the summation of all the psychological knowledge of antiquity.”

429. “Active imagination requires a state of reverie, half-way between sleep and waking.”

430. “Neurosis is always a substitute for legitimate suffering.”

431. “We don’t so much solve our problems as we outgrow them. We add capacities and experiences that eventually make us bigger than the problems.”

432. “If there is a fear of falling, the only safety consists in deliberately jumping.”

433. “There is no light without shadow, and no psychic wholeness without imperfection.”

434. “When you succeed in awakening the Kundalini, so that it starts to move out of its mere potentiality, you necessarily start a world which is totally different from our world. It is the world of eternity.”

---

435. “I don’t believe there is a God. I know there is a God.”

---

436. “Trust that which gives you meaning and accept it as your guide.”

---

437. “All the most powerful ideas in history go back to archetypes.”

---

438. "Just as we tend to assume that the world is as we see it, we naively suppose that people are as we imagine them to be."

439. "The unconscious process moves spiral-wise around a center, gradually getting closer, while the characteristics of the center grow more and more distinct."

440. "Medicines cure diseases, but only doctors can cure patients."

441. "All true things must change and only that which changes remains true."

442. "If a union is to take place between opposites like spirit and matter, conscious and unconscious, bright and dark, and so on, it will happen in a third thing, which represents not a compromise but something new."

443. "The world will ask you who you are, and if you don't know, the world will tell you."

444. "The capacity for inner dialogue is a touchstone for outer objectivity."

445. "The unexpected and the incredible belong in this world. Only then is life whole."

446. "Everyone can afford to give away a smile."

447. "Nothing affects the life of a child so much as the unlived life of its parent."

448. “We need more understanding of human nature, because the only real danger that exists is man himself.”

449. “The foundation of all mental illness is the unwillingness to experience legitimate suffering.”

450. “Resistance to the organized mass can be effected only by the man who is as well organized in his individuality as the mass itself.”

"What if I should discover that the poorest of the beggars and the most impudent of offenders are all
451. within me; and that I stand in need of the alms of my own kindness, that I, myself, am the enemy who must be loved – what then?"

"Nothing worse could happen to
452. one than to be completely understood."

453. "Man is the microcosm of the macrocosm ; the God on earth is built on the pattern of the God in nature. But the universal consciousness of the real Ego transcends a million fold the self-consciousness of the personal for false ego."

---

454. "So they speak soothingly about progress and the greatest possible happiness, forgetting that happiness is itself poisoned if the measure of suffering has not been fulfilled."

Made in the USA
Coppell, TX
17 January 2023

11201104R00090